D1126058

WITHDRAWN
FROM THE RECORDS OF
MID-CONTINENT
PUBLIC LIBRARY

J796.72 SCH13F
Schaefer, A. R.
Formula One cars

MID-CONTINENT PUBLIC LIBRARY
Liberty Branch
1000 Kent Street
Liberty, MO 64068

LI

Wild Rides!

Formula One Cars

By A. R. Schaefer

Consultant:
Betty Carlan
Research Librarian
International Motorsports Hall of Fame
Talladega, Alabama

Capstone *press*

Mankato, Minnesota

MID-CONTINENT PUBLIC LIBRARY
Liberty Branch
1000 Kent Street
Liberty, MO 64068

LI

MID-CONTINENT PUBLIC LIBRARY

3 0000 12545179 3

Edge Books are published by Capstone Press
151 Good Counsel Drive, P.O. Box 669, Mankato, Minnesota 56002
www.capstonepress.com

Copyright © 2005 by Capstone Press. All rights reserved.
No part of this publication may be reproduced in whole or in part, or stored in a retrieval
system, or transmitted in any form or by any means, electronic, mechanical,
photocopying, recording, or otherwise, without written permission of the publisher.
For information regarding permission, write to Capstone Press,
151 Good Counsel Drive, P.O. Box 669, Dept. R, Mankato, Minnesota 56002.
Printed in the United States of America

Library of Congress Cataloging-in-Publication Data
Schaefer, A. R. (Adam Richard), 1976–
    Formula One cars / by A. R. Schaefer.
    p. cm.—(Edge Books, Wild rides!)
    Includes bibliographical references and index.
    Contents: Formula One cars—Early Formula One cars—Designing a
    Formula One car—Formula One cars in competition.
    ISBN 0-7368-2724-2 (hardcover)
    1. Grand Prix racing—Juvenile literature. 2. Formula One automobiles—
Juvenile literature. [1. Automobile racing. 2. Grand Prix racing. 3. Formula One
automobiles.] I. Title. II. Series.
GV1029.S26 2005
796.72—dc22   2003027105

Summary: Discusses Formula One cars, including their history, design,
    and competitions.

Editorial Credits
Donald Lemke, editor; Kia Adams, series designer; Patrick D. Dentinger,
    book designer; Jo Miller, photo researcher; Eric Kudalis, product
    planning editor

Photo Credits
Getty Images/AFP/Stan Honda, 19; AFP/Toru Yamanaka, 4; Allsport UK, 16;
    Clive Mason, 14, 24–25; Clive Rose, cover; Hulton Archive, 8, 10, 13;
    Mark Thompson, 26; Mike Hewitt, 20–21; Nathan Lazarnick, 11
SportsChrome Inc./Bongarts, 28; Bongarts/Alexander-Hassenstein, 18;
    Bongarts/Martin-Rose, 17, 22; Sport the Library, 6

The publisher does not endorse products whose logos may appear on objects in
images in this book.

1 2 3 4 5 6 09 08 07 06 05 04

Table of Contents

Learn about:

- **Formula One racing**

- **Grand prix**

- **Formula One around the world**

CHAPTER **1**

Formula One Cars

A Formula One car zips around a corner and into a tunnel. The car travels so fast that the fans almost miss it. Engines roar and whine as other cars follow closely behind. One of the cars spins toward the corner. Wings on the car help the driver get traction and stay in control.

Around the next turn, the lead car makes a pit stop. The driver needs more fuel to finish the race. The pit crew works quickly. They refuel the car and check the tires for damage. When the crew is finished, they signal the driver. Within seconds, the driver is back on the track and still in the lead.

**During the Monaco Grand Prix, drivers race
Formula One cars through the streets.**

The cars continue to speed toward the end of the race. The fans at the track start cheering. After the final lap, the first car rushes across the finish line. The race marshal waves the checkered flag, and the crowd roars. The driver heads to the winner's circle.

Formula One Races

A Formula One (F1) race is called a grand prix. Almost all F1 races are 160 to 195 miles (260 to 315 kilometers) long.

Most F1 races are named for the country where they are held. The race in Indianapolis, Indiana, is called the United States Grand Prix. The F1 race in Montreal, Quebec, is called the Canadian Grand Prix.

Each grand prix course is different. During the Monaco Grand Prix, streets are blocked and drivers race through the city of Monte Carlo. The U.S. Grand Prix is run on a racetrack.

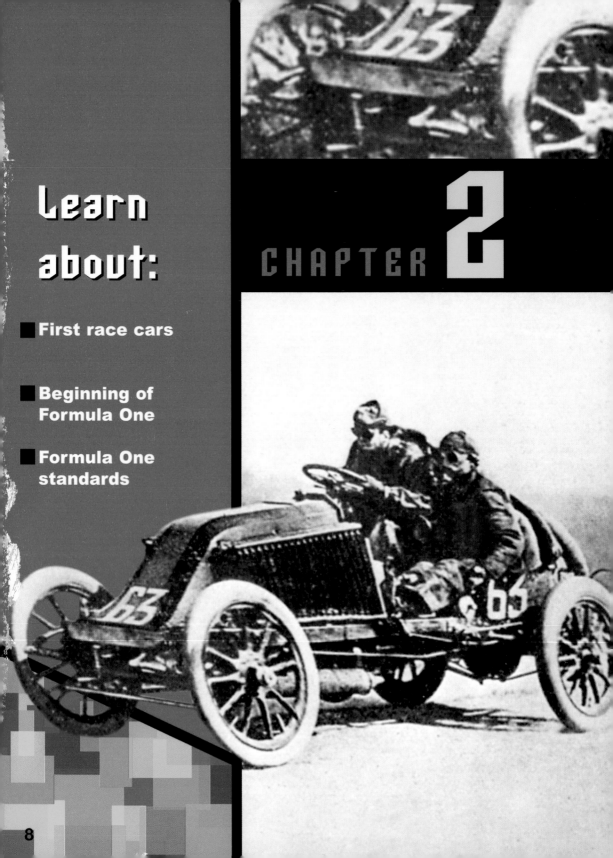

Learn about:

- **First race cars**

- **Beginning of Formula One**

- **Formula One standards**

CHAPTER **2**

Early Formula One Cars

For more than 100 years, people have raced open-wheel cars. These cars do not have fenders to cover the wheels. They include sprint cars, midgets, dragsters, and Indy cars. Today, the most popular open-wheel car is the Formula One.

Open-Wheel Racing

Open-wheel racing began in Europe in the late 1800s. Many of the early races were run between two cities. In 1895, the first road race was from Paris to Bordeaux, France, and back. The winner of this race averaged only 15 miles (24 kilometers) per hour.

In 1901, an open-wheel car sped through a city during a race from Paris, France, to Berlin, Germany.

Soon, open-wheel racing became more organized. In 1904, the Fédération Internationale de l'Automobile (FIA) formed in France. The FIA helped make racing safer for drivers and fans.

The FIA also helped put on races around the world. The first grand prix was near Le Mans, France, in 1906. In 1911, the first Indianapolis 500 took place in Indiana. It was the first major open-wheel race in the United States.

In 1911, many people came to Indiana to watch the first Indianapolis 500.

Early open-wheel race cars looked different than modern F1 cars. They were big and heavy, with square corners. These cars were designed to hold up under rough conditions. Many of the early racetracks were not paved. Sometimes, the winning speeds were less than 30 miles (50 kilometers) per hour.

Heavy cars were hard on tires. At a race in 1908, mechanics dug pits along the side of the track. Drivers could pull into these pits to have their tires changed. These stops became known as pit stops. Soon, pit stops became an important part of car racing.

Formula One

After World War II (1939–1945), open-wheel racing took off in Europe. The FIA started setting limits on engine size and body type. These limits were first known as Formula A standards. A few years later, they changed to Formula One.

By 1950, European carmakers were designing some of the fastest F1 cars. During that year, Italian driver Giuseppe Farina won the first Formula One World Championship. He drove an Alfa Romeo race car.

On May 1, 1950, Giuseppe Farina raced his Alfa Romeo at the Silverstone Race Circuit.

Learn about:

- **Downforce**

- **Stopping power**

- **Engine limits**

CHAPTER **3**

RENAULT

Designing a Formula One Car

Formula One cars are difficult to design. Each car takes months of planning and work. Ferrari, Jaguar, BMW, Mercedes, and other car companies have experienced race teams. Each racing team has designers, mechanics, and engineers. These people use the latest technology to design and build better F1 cars.

Building the Best

Before one season is over, designers are working on the next season's car. Sometimes, a race team will make only small changes to their car. Other times, they might need to build a completely new one.

After a car is designed on a computer, the team makes a model. They place this model in a wind tunnel. A wind tunnel tests the car's aerodynamics. Designers want to make sure every car moves through the air easily and quickly.

Wind tunnels help designers test the aerodynamics of Formula One cars.

Once the race team is happy with the model, they build the F1 car. The team tests this car and makes small changes before the racing season begins.

Formula One Wings

In the late 1960s, designers put wings on Formula One cars. Today, every F1 car has a front and rear wing. These wings create downforce. They push air down on the race car. This design gives the cars better traction. Drivers can travel fast around sharp corners with good traction. Wings also allow F1 cars to move through the air quickly.

Modern Formula One cars have a front wing and a rear wing.

Chassis

The frame of an F1 car is called a chassis. The chassis needs to be light and strong. Lightweight cars accelerate and stop faster than heavy cars. The chassis needs to be strong enough to travel at high speeds and make sharp turns. It also needs to protect the driver during a crash.

The frame of a Formula One car helps protect the driver.

Powerful Brakes

The brakes on F1 cars are similar to the brakes on regular cars. Discs are attached to the wheels. Two pads push into each disc when the driver is braking.

Formula One brakes are very powerful. They can slow a race car from 180 miles (290 kilometers) per hour to 50 miles (80 kilometers) per hour in less than 2 seconds.

Extreme braking can make the discs very hot. During races, the brake discs get so hot that they glow.

Tires

The tires on Formula One cars are different from those on regular cars. F1 tires can handle a great deal of force. But they last for only about 120 miles (190 kilometers).

Formula One cars need more than one set of tires during a race.

Most F1 tires don't last a whole race. Pit crews need to change the tires during pit stops. Race teams also change tires for different weather conditions.

Engines

The FIA sets limits on the size of F1 engines. These size limits can change from year to year. Even with these limits, F1 cars can travel very fast. In 2000, a car at the

Formula One cars perform in many types of weather, including rain.

Italian Grand Prix reached 221.1 miles (355.8 kilometers) per hour. This is the fastest speed ever recorded during an F1 race.

In the early 2000s, race teams used several engines during a race weekend. Many teams spent more than $1 million each week on engines. In 2004, a new rule limited teams to one engine per race weekend. Eventually, this rule might change again. It could limit teams to one engine for every six races.

Learn about:

- **Race weekend**

- **The grid**

- **Pit stops**

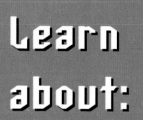

Formula One Cars in Competition

In 2003, the Formula One series held 16 races. These races took place in countries around the world. Each race had almost the same practice, qualifying, and racing rules.

Practice and Qualifying

Formula One racing events take place over a whole weekend. Fridays and Saturdays are practice and qualifying days. On Friday, drivers can run in two practice sessions. On Saturday, all drivers must run in a qualifying session.

The qualifying session has two parts. During the first part, each driver runs a qualifying lap. After everyone has driven in the first part, officials make a list. The list ranks the drivers from fastest to slowest.

During the second part, the slowest driver runs the qualifying lap first. The driver with the fastest time goes last. After everyone has finished, race officials make another list. This list ranks each driver in order of their second time. Officials use the list to make the grid.

The grid shows the starting order for the race on Sunday. The fastest car has the pole position. The driver of this car starts on the inside of the first row. The next fastest driver starts a little behind to the right. The third fastest driver will be on the inside of the second row.

Formula One cars race away from the starting line during the Australian Grand Prix on March 4, 2001.

The Race

Officials open the track a half hour before the race starts. Drivers can take a practice lap before the race. After the practice lap, drivers take their places behind the starting line.

Pit crews change tires and refuel Formula One cars.

Drivers start their engines one minute before the grand prix begins. Then, the drivers take one slow lap around the course. They follow a safety car, also known as the pace car. At the end of the pace lap, five red lights come on one at a time. The lights shut off to signal the start of the race.

During the race, drivers come into the pits for new tires, fuel, and minor repairs. Pit crews work quickly to service the car. Other cars on the track can move ahead while a car is in the pits.

When there is one lap left in the race, the marshal waves a white flag. The cars race to the finish line. The first car to reach the line wins first prize.

Michael Schumacher

In 1994, Michael Schumacher won his first Formula One championship. He was only 26 years old. Schumacher became the second-youngest driver to win the championship. Soon, he would become one of the best Formula One drivers of all time.

Schumacher was born in Germany in 1969. In 1991, he drove in his first Formula One race. The next year, he won his first F1 race at the Belgian Grand Prix. In 1995, he won nine races and his second championship.

After the 1995 season, Schumacher switched from the Benneton team to the Ferrari team. He was still a successful driver. In 2002, Schumacher won 11 out of 17 races. In 2003, he won his sixth championship title.

Glossary

accelerate (ak-SEL-uh-rate)—to gain speed or speed up

aerodynamic (air-oh-dye-NA-mik)—designed to move through the air easily and quickly

chassis (CHASS-ee)—the frame on which the body of a vehicle is built

downforce (DOUN-forss)—pressure applied in a downward direction as a car moves forward; downforce improves a car's traction.

grand prix (GRAND PREE)—one of a series of Formula One car races

marshal (MAR-shuhl)—a course official who oversees the safe running of a race

pit (PIT)—the area of a racetrack where cars go to be refueled and repaired

pole position (POHL puh-ZISH-uhn)—the first spot in the race grid; the fastest qualifying car starts in the pole position.

traction (TRAK-shuhn)—the gripping power or friction that keeps a vehicle from slipping on the road

Read More

Fox, Martha Capwell. *Car Racing.* History of Sports. San Diego: Lucent Books, 2004.

Herran, Joe, and Ron Thomas. *Formula One Car Racing.* Action Sports. Philadelphia: Chelsea House, 2003.

Pitt, Matthew. *Formula One.* Built for Speed. New York: Children's Press, 2001.

Internet Sites

FactHound offers a safe, fun way to find Internet sites related to this book. All of the sites on FactHound have been researched by our staff.

Here's how:

1. Visit *www.facthound.com*

2. Type in this special code **0736827242** for age-appropriate sites. Or enter a search word related to this book for a more general search.

3. Click on the **Fetch It** button.

FactHound will fetch the best sites for you!

Index